# Caviar

A TRUE DELICACY

**SUSIE BOECKMANN &
NATALIE REBEIZ-NIELSEN**

MACMILLAN•USA

## Notes

Standard level spoon measurements are used in all recipes.

Eggs should be medium unless otherwise stated.

Milk should be whole milk unless otherwise stated.

All butter is sweet unless otherwise stated.

Ovens should be preheated to the specified temperature – if using a fan-assisted oven follow the manufacturer's instructions for adjusting the time and the temperature.

Art Director: **Jacqui Small**

Executive Art Editor: **Penny Stock**

Executive Editor: **Susan Haynes**

Editor: **Sasha Judelson**

Photography: **James Merrell**

Stylist: **Sue Skeen**

Home Economist: **Bridget Sargeson**

MACMILLAN
A Simon and Schuster Macmillan Company
1633 Broadway
New York, NY 10019-6785
First published in 1995 by Reed Consumer Books Limited.

**Library of Congress Cataloging-in-Publication Data
available.**

ISBN 0-02-860375-3

Produced by Mandarin Offset
Printed and bound in China

10 9 8 7 6 5 4 3 2 1

Our heartfelt thanks go to Hanne Sorensen who coordinated and kept us under control, always with a smile; to all those in Caviar House who gave us their support and information, and to all the other people in the caviar industry who helped contribute; to Dr. Alwyne Wheeler, formerly of the British Museum (Natural History) and finally to our patient husbands and children. Hopefully you will find our dishes attractive and delicious, to tickle your taste buds without making your pockets too bare.

## CONTENTS

Introduction **7**

Caviar Curiosities **8**

Appearances **13**

Caviar Varieties **15**

How to Serve Caviar **20**

What to Drink with Caviar **22**

A Little Guidance **24**

The Recipes **27**

Index **64**

# INTRODUCTION

There are now three main kinds of caviar sold commercially, although there are over 400 different species of sturgeon worldwide. It is only in the Caspian that the unique combination of optimum water temperatures, climate and rivers running into the sea come together to create the perfect conditions for this fish; the caviar of the Caspian sturgeon is acknowledged to be the best in the world. There are many other parts of the world where caviar is produced, but it never consistently equals the quality of the Caspian variety.

The largest of the fish is the Beluga, followed by the Oscietre and then the Sevruga. Not long ago there were also Sterlet and Schipp, but these two are no longer caught in sufficient quantities to be sold commercially. There is also the very rare golden caviar (generally agreed to be the Albino Oscietre or Beluga), which it was the right of the czars of Russia and the shahs of Iran to consume. Any commoner caught eating this rare delicacy in Iran was liable to lose his right hand! Today we can sometimes obtain this type of caviar but it is very rare, and therefore extremely expensive.

The sturgeon is a migratory fish, generally swimming up river to spawn and returning to the sea every year, although there are exceptions to this: some sturgeon have adapted to staying solely in rivers or the sea. Many sturgeon species interbreed with each other, which has sometimes made identifying different species rather difficult.

The spurned wife of a movie mogul in Hollywood took to bathing in caviar when her husband fell for a beautiful young actress. Her first reason for doing this was that she really believed that caviar would keep her skin soft and youthful; the second was that she paid with his credit card, which gave her an even bigger boost!

# CAVIAR CURIOSITIES

### Russian Caviar

Russian caviar has always had a wonderful reputation. In 1893 the Russians made an agreement with Iran to purchase, process and import all the Iranian sturgeon catch. This resulted in the Iranians being forced to sell to the Russians at greatly reduced prices until 1952, when the parties agreed fishing rights and became independent producers.

Unfortunately, since the dissolution of the U.S.S.R. there has been a breakdown in controlling the previously strict quotas on sturgeon catches. The State no longer controls the caviar market, making sure that it is produced in prime condition. This has led to a great deal of poaching and illegal fishing.

Powerful local mafias have gained control of the fishing stations in many areas because caviar is such a valuable commodity and is dealt in much desired Western currencies. Consequently, those in the established caviar industry often come across eggs that are not properly cleaned or preserved and, moreover, are sold in fake cans designed to resemble the official state packaging.

Despite attempts to prevent overfishing, such as the two frigates and 300 soldiers patrolling the Volga tributeries, the Beluga is nearly extinct; if controls are not brought in soon, it will cease to exist.

This once famous Russian delicacy has recently been overtaken by Iran, which now produces a fine quality product in modern factories and to Western health standards.

### Is there any difference between Russian and Iranian Caviar?

The fish are caught in the same sea but there are differences in the processing of the caviar. Russian caviar tends to have more salt added than Iranian, and the Russians add a little borax to the salt, which enhances the flavor, preserves the caviar for longer and sweetens the eggs a little. This also makes the eggs a bit oilier.

The Iranians process with pure salt at around 1.15 percent a pound as opposed to 1.8 percent a pound in Russia.

### History

The sturgeon is a prehistoric fish; fossil remains dating from that time have been found on the Baltic coast and elsewhere.

Around 2400 BC the ancient Egyptian and Phoenician coastal dwellers knew how to salt and pickle fish and eggs, to last them in times of war, famine or on long sea voyages. There are some bas-reliefs at the Necropolis near the Sakkara Pyramid that show fisherman catching all kinds of fish, gutting them and removing their eggs.

Writing in the fourth century BC, Aristotle declared sturgeon flesh delicious and described how a gelatin made from the swim bladder was used as a strong glue and for clarifying wine. (It is called isinglas and is still used today for these same purposes, and also in optics; the Chinese dry the product for use in soup.) When Rome was at the height of its prosperity from the fourth century BC onwards, many writers and philosophers, including Pliny, Cicero, Ovid and Athenaeus, wrote of sturgeon.

In the Middle Ages shoals of sturgeon were to be found in the Thames, Seine, Po and Ebro rivers and the upper stretches of the Danube. At this time sovereigns of many countries, including Russia, China, Denmark, France and England, had claimed the rights to sturgeon. Fishermen had to offer the catch to the sovereign, often for fixed rewards.

In Russia and Hungary the sections of rivers considered suitable for fishing the great sturgeon (the Beluga as we know it) were the subject of special royal grants. Under the czar's benevolence, the Cossacks of the Dnieper, the Don and the Ural were allowed to fish for one two-week period twice a year, in the spring (Bagornaja catch) and fall (Plawnaja catch).

Apart from the Cossacks and their families, the river banks were crowded with rich dealers from Moscow, Leningrad and parts of Europe. The fresh fish were sold to the highest bidder, who then had the fish killed, prepared the caviar on the spot, and then packed it in barrels filled with ice to be transported. The Cossacks continued to have the right to sturgeon fishing until the Russian Revolution in 1917.

## Aphrodite's Eggs

Aphrodite is the Goddess of Love. Coming from the sea, she epitomizes love, passion and health, making caviar and other seafood the ideal food for lovers. It should be treated as such.

There's no scientific proof that caviar is an aphrodisiac, but its stimulating properties are incontestable – from old Russian poetry to ancient Persian and Indian stories, caviar has always been lauded for its "exciting virtues" in seduction.

## Health and Nutrition

Caviar is light, full of vitamins, low in calories and almost a complete food in itself.

Russia has known of the health benefits of caviar for centuries, and it is used today to prevent rickets in children. It is also given to patients after surgery to aid their recovery, because, in addition to its high protein content, it is easy to consume and digest. Caviar is believed to increase the life span of the consumer.

Caviar is also good for hangovers, as it contains acetylcholine, which increases tolerance to alcohol. Russians extract the oil from the eggs and drink it as we might drink cod liver oil, and use it to line their stomachs before hitting the vodka.

## Beauty Treatments

Some people like to bathe in caviar, and it has been used as a beauty product by several cosmetic companies.

Beauticians have been known to use caviar for a nourishing face mask by extracting the essential oils from the eggs. The testes of the male sturgeon is made into a balm to soothe and cure burns.

A Manhattan hair salon made a solution of caviar and clay to condition dry bleached hair. It was said to be very popular. Bloomingdales stocks a caviar-extract rejuvenating cream for the eyes and throat, which is sold at $35 for half an ounce! A pharmacist in London also once extracted the oils from caviar and mixed them to a secret formula that he marketed as a rejuvenating cream.

A Scotsman dining at the Waldorf Astoria for the first time, with a new girl-friend asked what was the most expensive dish on the menu. The waiter replied "Caviar, Sir" – "What is that?" inquired the man. "Fish eggs, Sir" – "We will have one each, fried sunny side up, waiter" ordered the careful gentleman.

# APPEARANCES

## Good

**Cans** should be vacuum-packed with a tight seal. To break the seal it should be necessary to use a coin on the can's edge to break the vacuum. Any rubber bands on cans should be removed with a knife. Lift the lid carefully – the can should be firmly packed with eggs.

**Caviar** should have a healthy, glossy, slightly oily appearance. The eggs should all be separate, round and firm (but not hard).

**Smell** your eggs – there should be a slight aroma of the sea, never a strong odor.

**To** taste, put a little caviar on the back of your hand in the "V" between your thumb and forefinger. Eat it from the skin, rolling the eggs in your mouth and then gently popping them to release their full flavor (which will vary from variety to variety and fish to fish). Then rub the skin on your hand; there should be no remaining smell.

**If** your caviar has been frozen, you can try a rescue job. Either thaw it slowly in the refrigerator or transfer the eggs to a fine non-metal (preferably silk-meshed) strainer.

**When** buying good caviar packed in glass, turn the jar around slowly: the eggs should follow the jar around.

**If** you buy caviar from a good retailer (unless you are buying the original blue 4-pound cans) you will usually find that Beluga is in blue-labeled cans, Oscietre in yellow, and Sevruga in red.

**Cans** of caviar can be kept in a refrigerator for about 2–3 months at a temperature of 37°F. A professional will keep cans for up to a year at a temperature of between 26°F and 22°F. Larger cans should be turned from time to time to redistribute the natural oils evenly.

## Bad

**The** vacuum seal should never be broken. This would mean that the can was not properly sealed, allowing air to get in and destroy the eggs. It could also mean that the can had been opened by someone else, either to repack the contents or even to change them to something other than that specified on the lid. The can should always be full (regardless of size); if it is not, the contents are likely to have been incorrectly packed or processed.

**If** there is anything other than eggs and a little oil in your caviar – such as bits of membrane, specks of blood or white crystals around the eggs – return the can to the retailer immediately.

**If** the eggs smell tart, acidic or fishy, they are not fresh.

**When** caviar is old it becomes much saltier. If eggs have a strong fishy flavor or slight ammonia-like taste, they are not fresh.

**If** caviar does not move around the jar, be suspicious – it is probably low grade, too old, and has become dry.

**Black**-market caviar can come in any can, although the packaging will usually resemble that used for well-known brands.

**Never** open a can of caviar without checking the sell-by date.

**Glass** jars often have a magnifying effect on eggs, so your eggs may look bigger than they actually are.

In the United States at the beginning of this century, before prohibition, there was such an abundance of caviar that it was given away free in New York bars to encourage greater beer consumption, being rather salty.

# CAVIAR VARIETIES

The three prominent varieties of caviar sold are Beluga, Sevruga and Oscietre, and these are the varieties you are most likely to eat and buy. We discuss these caviars on the next page, together with Golden or Imperial caviar. The caviars produced from other sturgeon are interesting to compare to the main caviars in terms of flavor and production methods. Many countries produce fake eggs using fish products with oils, gelatin and flavorings. By using dyes and artificial flavorings the color and taste of an egg can be regulated to resemble almost any fish egg from salmon to sturgeon.

## STERLET

### (Acipenser ruthenus Linnaeus)

The Sterlet is similar to but smaller than the average Sevruga. It has been known to reach 4 feet and weigh as much as 35 pounds, but normally the fish does not grow to more than 39 inches in length and weighs 13–14 pounds.

In the past Sterlet (mainly a river sturgeon) accounted for over 50 percent of the catch from the mouth of the Volga. Fifty years ago 700 tons were caught in a year, but now it is very rare.

The largest remaining population of the Sterlet is in the former Yugoslavia, then Bulgaria, Romania, the Czech Republic, Slovakia and Hungary. Although it is no longer caught for commercial caviar purposes, the Sterlet is a very important fish as far as propagation is concerned, breeding and crossbreeding successfully in warm water with other species of sturgeon. This fact makes it a vital member of the sturgeon family for the future. Historically, the Sterlet has featured in all kinds of feasts and banquets; Sterlet caviar soup seems to have been popular.

## SCHIPP CAVIAR

This is sometimes sold commercially. The flavor is somewhere between Sevruga and Oscietre, but the eggs are often less firm than either of these. Sometimes the eggs are graded as Oscietre or Sevruga, depending on the size caught. Schipp is the result of crossbreeding between the Sterlet and Sevruga.

## PRESSED CAVIAR

Pressed caviar is compressed eggs mainly taken from damaged Sevruga or Oscietre sturgeon, resulting in a strong salty, fishy flavor. It is not so popular today but is highly appreciated by traditional caviar experts and is easy to cook with.

## MALOSSOL

The word "malossol" means lightly salted in Russian and traditionally only eggs in prime condition are prepared and labeled this way. It takes great expertise to judge precisely the stage at which a sturgeon's eggs are absolutely right for this process, so beware! The eggs may not contain more than 2.8–3 percent salt. In Europe a very small amount of borax is added to the salt (many experts believe this improves and slightly sweetens the caviar), but this is not permitted in the United States. Iran also uses only pure salt for processing.

"Malossol" has wrongly come to mean any high quality caviar.

## PASTEURIZED CAVIAR

Russia went into pasteurizing caviar seriously around the time of the First World War, and remains the only country to produce it. It was so cold then that fishing became impossible. Rather than lose their established markets, the Russians poured their existing stocks of caviar into huge 104–gallon barrels, covered the tops and left them in a very hot room to cook.

Today's methods are much more effective: jars of caviar are properly sealed and put into water baths with a constant temperature of about 140°F.

The glass jars commonly used to package pasteurized caviar can have the effect of magnifying the eggs when viewed from the outside, which is why so much is falsely sold as Beluga.

## CHINESE CAVIAR

There are several species of sturgeon found in China, mainly in the Amur and Liman rivers. Most commonly known as the Kaluga, the eggs are, unfortunately, often very salty and, because of the fishing methods used, do not have consistent quality.

## GOLDEN OR IMPERIAL CAVIAR

Golden caviar used to be reserved for the czars of
Russia, emperors of Manchuria and even the Vatican.
In the recent past in Iran it was kept exclusively for
the Shah.

Caviar experts have many theories as to what golden
caviar actually is. The biggest caviar company
believes that golden caviar comes from an Oscietre
fish that is over 60 years old. At that point the eggs
change to a pale golden color and the flavor
becomes smooth, creamy and delicate.

Another popular theory is that golden caviar comes
from an albino fish – Beluga or Oscietre (and in the
past from the Sterlet as well). The eggs are an off-
white color. Albino caviar commands a very high
price because of its rarity. The flavor is not nearly as
good as that of the pale Oscietre eggs.

**Pictured right**

### OSCIETRE
*(Acipencer guldenstadtii)*

The Oscietre sturgeon is in some ways the most
interesting of the sturgeon, as it has the widest
variety of eggs in terms of size, color and taste. The
average mature fish grows to 4¾ feet and weighs
between 44 and 176 pounds. It has a short thick
head with a slightly pointed nose and a small mouth
through which it sucks up plants, small fish and
crustaceans. It also has two sets of barbels above its
mouth; these are important feelers when the fish is
feeding on the bottom of the seabed.

The Oscietre starts producing eggs from the age of
12. When it is young, the eggs are large and mostly
of a dark golden shade. As the fish ages the roe fades
to a pale amber and has a subtler flavor. Some say
that the taste differs so much because the fish dives
to the sea-bottom to avoid fishermen. It buries itself
under algae and mud. The camouflage it chooses
may affect the flavor.

**Pictured left**

## BELUGA
*(Huso huso)*

The Beluga is the biggest of the sturgeons and the only one that is exclusively carnivorous. It is so rare that it is unusual for more than 100 to be caught per year in the Caspian waters.

The Beluga is a silvery gray color and differs from other sturgeon in that it loses the bony scales along its length when it is a few months old. It has a big, short head with a pointed snout and large mouth and two sets of barbels under its mouth.

The mouth of a full-grown Beluga sturgeon may be up to 10 inches wide, and the fish has been known to swallow whole salmon. It is also the fastest swimmer of the sturgeon family, enabling it to follow shoals of shad, herring, mullet and other white fish.

Up to 25 percent of the Beluga's body weight may consist of eggs, but individual fish have been known to carry up to 50 percent of their weight in eggs. The female fish matures only when it is 25–40 years old, and may not spawn every year.

The female Beluga is highly prized for its large grained egg with a fine skin. The color varies from light gray to nearly black. The lightest gray is particularly prized.

**Pictured right**

## SEVRUGA
*(Acipenser stellatus)*

The Sevruga is the smallest sturgeon used commercially. It grows to a maximum of 4¾ feet and seldom exceeds 55 pounds. It has a snub nose with a long snout and two sets of barbels just above its small mouth. Like the Oscietre, it is an omnivore and bottom-feeds on algae and crustaceans. It has very distinctive bony scales, which resemble stars. The female Sevruga starts producing eggs from about 7 to 10 years of age; around 10–12 percent of her body weight are eggs. Most of the fish caught are 8–22 years old, when the eggs are probably at their best. The eggs are gray-black with a fine grain. They are small and the most salty to taste. Among connoisseurs they are highly appreciated for their unique flavor. They are also the least expensive source of caviar, mainly because there are more of them and they produce eggs at an earlier age.

**Pictured left**

## EGGS FROM OTHER SOURCES

Other fish eggs eaten include cod, herring, flying fish, pike, carp, pollack, flounder, mackerel and some species of crab. In most countries fish eggs should be labeled caviar only if they come from sturgeon from the Caspian Sea, but there are exceptions to this and some countries, including America, use the word caviar together with the name of the fish that yielded the roe, such as lumpfish caviar or salmon caviar.

## SALMON EGGS/KETA

These are large, naturally orange-red colored eggs about the size of a small pea. They have a strong salmon, "yolky" flavor and should melt in the mouth. The eggs should be a good round shape and should not break when squeezed. There is not much difference between pasteurized and unpasteurized salmon eggs.

Several kinds of salmon are used for their eggs but the most common are keta in Europe and chum, pink or sockeye in America. Japan and Russia are by far the largest producers and consumers of salmon eggs in the world.
**Pictured right**

## FISH EGGS (AMERICAN)

These come from a variety of fish. They can be natural, colored or flavored, according to market requirements.
**Pictured left**

## LUMPFISH

This fish is found mainly in Scandinavian waters. It weighs between 4 and 15 pounds; some 15–30 percent of its body weight consists of eggs. The eggs are a small-grain roe, which come in a rainbow of colors. They are normally dyed dark gray or black to resemble Sevruga caviar, or sometimes red. Lumpfish roe is widely used as a garnish for soups and canapés instead of "real" caviar. It has a slightly fishy, salty taste and is slightly crunchy to eat.

## MULLET EGGS

These are the oldest recorded dried and processed eggs, predating sturgeon. Today they are still widely sold as *Botarga* (the spelling varies). The eggs are salted, dried and then preserved in a translucent wax casing.

## TROUT EGGS

The smaller grained orange eggs of the trout are about half the size of salmon eggs. Enthusiastic anglers take the eggs from the trout they catch, wash the roe in milk, then rinse it in water several times. They add salt and a little sugar before draining the roe as much as possible on paper towels, then placing it in a bowl to be pressed with a weight for 24 hours.
Pressed roe spread on toast is quite delicious.
**Pictured right**

## TUNA EGGS

In America albacore tuna is caught off both coasts and bonito is caught in Pacific waters. Spawning occurs from April to June when the water becomes warmer. Tuna eggs are vacuum-packed to retain their taste and fragrance. They should be taken out of their container a couple of hours before serving.

## SEA URCHIN EGGS

The most expensive seafood eggs come from *oursin,* a type of black, spiny sea urchin considered a great delicacy among fish-eating connoisseurs. The *oursin* is now a protected species in some Mediterranean waters. It is collected in the summer months in deep, rocky waters and when cut open reveals a bright orange mass of very small eggs, which have a very delicate taste and fine, slightly grainy texture.

## AMERICAN CAVIAR

This comes mainly from the farmed paddlefish (not a true sturgeon). There are strict laws regarding processing and selling. It has a poor flavor compared with Caspian caviar.
**Pictured left**

There are several other species of sturgeon and fish eggs that we have not covered, as you are not likely to come across them in commercial or retail outlets.

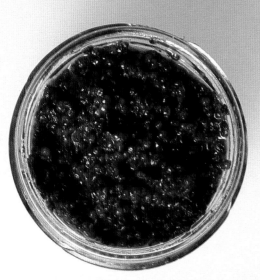

# HOW TO SERVE CAVIAR

Of course, you can eat your caviar from a simple glass bowl, using a plastic spoon, but artists through history have been inspired by the rarity and expense of caviar. Fabergé created spoons of gold, malachite, lapis lazuli and amber; others were inspired to use mother-of-pearl, tortoise shell and polished wood. Two early gold and silversmiths, Paul de Lamerie and Paul Storr, each designed and made beautiful solid silver caviar servers with inner dishes lined in gold. Old Russian and French silversmiths have also paid homage to caviar – even Louis Vuitton has a marvelous caviar picnic set. Lalique also has some fine examples of caviar dishes in its exquisite glass.

Today you can find spoons, scoops and caviar knives made of mother-of-pearl, wood or horn (usually deer, cattle or ram's horn). They come in many sizes and shapes and should be as smooth as your caviar! Some are simple, others carved or with handles decorated in silver or gold.

Horn spoons are used most often today and to retain their lustre they should not be washed in dishwashers or with hot water or detergents. Wipe clean with vinegar and paper towels, rinse under warm water and dry carefully.

## Notes on Serving

Take your caviar out of the refrigerator 10 minutes to 1 hour before serving, but do not actually open the can or jar until the last minute.

Remember caviar's enemies – air and heat!

Use bone, mother-of-pearl, gold plated or even plastic spoons – never use stainless steel or silver or your caviar will rapidly change its flavor and oxidize. Plastic is better than metal because (unlike many more exotic and attractive materials) it does not carry a taste, is unaffected by acids, vinegar or oils and does not stain.

If you have a special caviar dish, put crushed ice in the outer bowl, keep it chilled and add the caviar at the last minute. If you do not have a special caviar serving bowl, you can simply put the can or jar in a glass bowl of crushed ice. Scoop caviar out of the can vertically from top to bottom, never horizontally, as this might crush the grains.

Serve directly on individual plates.

Caviar should never be exposed to the air for more than 1 hour.

## How much do you need?

Allow 1–2 ounces – 3–5 teaspoons – of caviar per person. It is quite a good idea to buy the amount you require in two cans rather than purchasing one large can, just in case you do not use it all. If unopened, the second container can be kept for another occasion. This makes sense because once opened, caviar must be consumed within two or three days and, after all, there are some people who do not like it (more for us!).

# WHAT TO DRINK WITH CAVIAR

The Russians are the largest consumers of caviar and vodka is the national drink, so this creates a natural bond between the two – both for celebrations and for every day. There is a large choice of excellent vodkas to be found at good wine merchants today. They will advise you, or you can experiment with different flavors. One of the most popular vodkas sold in Natalie's shop is pepper–flavored. Otherwise go for a classic Stolichnaya.

Vodka should be served very cold. If you keep your vodka in the freezer, it will not freeze because of the alcohol content, but when poured it will come out like a syrup.

Some people prefer a champagne or a dry white wine. A good crisp white burgundy such as a Chablis or a Pouilly Fuisse or Fumé is delicious with caviar, as are some of the New World Chardonnays, but avoid the really oaky ones, which are too rich and fruity for caviar.

As caviar is normally served as an event, to seduce, to impress, or just because you like it, it is important to have the drink that you enjoy the most. As with caviar, always follow your personal taste.

**The number of caviar cans or glass jars packed per year is approximately 1,100,000.**

# A LITTLE GUIDANCE

There are many misconceptions regarding caviar and one of the commonest questions asked is: "Which is the best?"

To people in the caviar business that is really like asking if you prefer sole, salmon or trout – it depends on your choice or the prevailing circumstances: perhaps your dealer has a better Oscietre than Sevruga on the date of purchase or vice versa.

It would be unwise to put Beluga on canapés at a large reception, as the delicate flavor would probably not be appreciated by a chatty group of people consuming a variety of drinks in a crowded room. On the other hand, a romantic dinner for two would be an ideal occasion to enjoy the creamy delicate flavor.

With its stronger flavor, Sevruga is excellent on small canapés.

Many people also insist that "a black Beluga with very large eggs" is the best, whereas others state with equal conviction that gray is the only good color. There really is no difference in the quality. The color of the eggs comes from the individual fish.

Caviar should be judged by its quality and taste and not by the price. People tend to think that the most expensive is the best, but this is not necessarily true. Many connoisseurs would prize a new season Sevruga with its long distinctive nose, small eggs, and delicate but strongish flavor above all others.

**The Queen's Grill on the *Queen Elizabeth 2* serves 15 percent of the world's consumption of Beluga caviar.**

# THE RECIPES

The best way to eat good caviar is by itself with perhaps thin white toast, blinis or waxy new potatoes, but because it is rare and expensive we have tried to create a selection of different dishes to suit every occasion and have not used any recipes that we don't like ourselves. With all the recipes we suggest, you can, of course, change the type of caviar to suit your taste, pocket or gift. The only proviso is that if you are adding caviar to a hot sauce, Sevruga eggs are the most suitable, as they can withstand a certain amount of cooking. Beluga eggs are too delicate and will burst and leave your dish a rather muddy color. If you are enclosing eggs in a dish, you can get away with an Oscietre, as the center of the dish is not cooked for long enough to destroy the caviar in the middle.

You do not have to be tied to most recipes — fromage frais, sour cream or crème fraîche — it is simply a question of what you prefer. Be aware, however, that sour cream is usually runnier than the other two, so for coating or spreading on a canapé, it is better to use crème fraîche or fromage frais.

We do not feel that lemon juice should be added to any caviar except pasteurized caviar, because it can oxidize the eggs.

For many people the perfect combination is a baked potato and caviar. You can create this dish with potatoes of any size. Bake the potatoes in a preheated oven, at 350°F for 1–2 hours, depending on their size. Split the potatoes down the center and squeeze to open them up. Spoon crème fraîche or sour cream into the center of each. Sprinkle with chopped red onion and top with caviar.

# CAVIAR

## WITH TRADITIONAL ACCOMPANIMENTS & BLINIS

This way of serving caviar probably originated in Europe and America, supposedly introduced to mask the taste of rancid or salty caviar. Although it is no longer necessary to take such steps, it does make your caviar go further. Some stores and supermarkets that sell caviar now sell blinis.

**2 eggs**

**2 tablespoons of finely chopped parsley**

**1 large red onion, very finely chopped**

**4–5 teaspoons caviar of your choice per person**

**⅔ cup sour cream**

**1 lemon, quartered (optional)**

First make your blinis, following the recipe of your choice (see pages 30–31). These may be made in advance and kept covered in the refrigerator or frozen until about 1 hour before using. Heat just before serving. Put the eggs in a saucepan of cold, salted water. Bring to the boil, reduce the heat and simmer for 10 minutes, then drain, cool under cold running water and drain again. Set aside.

Shell the eggs and carefully remove the yolks. Chop both whites and yolks finely, keeping them separate. Arrange the hard-cooked egg whites, yolks, parsley and onion around the rim of four individual plates, leaving the center free for the caviar, which should be added just before serving. The sour cream may be put on the plate or passed around in a bowl. If you must, add a lemon wedge to each portion.

Pass around the warm blinis, allowing several per person, depending on the size.

Serves 4

**In Russia caviar was perfectly commonplace;
the czar's children used to eat
mashed banana and caviar for breakfast.**

# BLINI

Nice and easy for busy working people; you do not need a blini pan to make these big thick blinis.

**1¾ cups all-purpose flour, sifted**

**¼ teaspoon salt**

**3 eggs**

**1¾ cups 2% milk**

**¼ cup/½ stick butter**

**caviar, to serve**

Prepare the batter. Combine the flour, salt, eggs and milk in a blender or food processor. Process for 1–2 minutes until smooth. Alternatively, combine the dry ingredients in a large bowl, make a well in the center and add the beaten eggs and milk to the well. Gradually incorporate the flour, stirring until smooth. Whichever method you choose, strain the batter into a pitcher and let it stand for 30 minutes.

Melt the butter in a small saucepan, and pour a little into a large nonstick skillet. Pour enough of the batter into the pan to make four blinis (small pancakes), each about ¼ inch thick. Allow them to cook for about 10 minutes on each side over a moderate heat.

When the blinis are cooked, transfer them to a wire rack, piling them loosely on top of each other to keep them moist. Keep them warm in a low oven while making four more blinis, remembering to add a little more melted butter to the pan when necessary.

Serve the blinis warm, with caviar.

Makes 8

# BLINI WITH BUCKWHEAT

1–1¼ cups milk

1½ teaspoons dry yeast or 1 heaping teaspoon fresh yeast

¼ cup lukewarm water, if using fresh yeast

½ cup all-purpose flour

¾ heaping cup buckwheat flour

½ teaspoon salt

¼ cup/½ stick butter (maybe a bit more when cooking blinis)

2 eggs, separated

2 tablespoons sour cream

caviar, to serve

Pour ¼ cup of the milk into a pan. Heat over moderate heat until the milk rises to the brim of the pan, remove from the heat and allow to cool. Mix the fresh yeast with the water. Leave for 5 minutes until the surface is covered in bubbles. Sift the flours and salt into a bowl. Mix thoroughly. Add the dry yeast, then make a well, or make a well and add the fresh yeast. Add lukewarm milk to the well. Gradually incorporate the flour. Beat for 2 minutes until smooth. Cover with a damp dish towel and put in a warm place for 2–3 hours until risen and full of bubbles. Melt half the butter in a saucepan and allow to cool a little. Add a further ¼ cup of the milk to the risen batter and stir it in thoroughly. Stir in the egg yolks, sour cream and melted butter until the mixture has the consistency of heavy cream. (If it seems too thick to pour, add a little more milk.) Whisk the egg whites until stiff peaks form. Fold the egg whites into the batter, a little at a time, cutting and folding into the batter until thoroughly mixed in. Heat half the remaining butter in a skillet. Pour enough batter into the pan to make small blinis. Cook for 1–2 minutes, turning when lightly browned. Add more butter to the pan as necessary until all the batter is used. Serve warm, with caviar.

Serves 8

# TÊTE-À-TÊTE

This romantic breakfast for "the morning after" is highly nutritious, full of protein and should

heighten your energy buzz enormously.

**2 very fresh eggs**

**2 heaping teaspoons sour cream or fromage frais**

**3 teaspoons caviar**

**thinly sliced white bread, cut into strips**

Boil the eggs for 4 minutes. Remove the tops of the shells with a sharp knife, transfer the eggs to egg cups

and spoon 1 teaspoon of sour cream or fromage frais into each.

Add 1½ teaspoons of caviar to each egg and serve immediately with strips of thin white bread (toasted if

preferred). Also have available freshly squeezed orange juice and pink champagne.

Serves 2

### Variation
# THE SOPHISTICATED DINNER VERSION

Carefully saw the tops off four eggs, empty the contents of the shells into a bowl. Carefully wash out the

eggshells and dry or drain on paper towels. Place the dry shells into egg cups.

Beat the eggs together and then strain to remove any particles of shell or other bits.

Pour the egg mixture into a nonstick saucepan and over a low heat whisk until the eggs thicken slightly.

Remove the pan from the heat. Stirring continuously, add salt and pepper, 2 teaspoons of fromage frais or

sour cream, 1 teaspoon of chopped onion and 1 teaspoon of finely chopped chives. Fill each eggshell with

the cooked egg mixture until three-quarters full. Add 1½ teaspoons of caviar to each egg and pop the

eggshell tops on top. Serve with wedges of thin white toast.

Serves 4

# SCRAMBLED EGGS WITH CAVIAR

This makes a delicious brunch dish or dinner party appetizer. It can be served in ramekins as we suggest here or directly on a plate, whichever suits the occasion.

**2 tablespoons/¼ stick butter**

**6 eggs**

**I generous tablespoon heavy cream**

**4 teaspoons Sevruga caviar**

**salt and pepper**

Heat four ramekins in a low oven. In a nonstick saucepan gently heat the butter. Place the eggs in a bowl with seasoning to taste – add salt sparingly, as the caviar will be salty. Whisk until frothy, add to the pan and increase the heat slightly. Stir with a wooden spoon until the eggs begin to thicken. Then add the cream. Remove the pan from the heat, still stirring to obtain a thick but creamy consistency. (Adding cream at the end of cooking stops the eggs becoming overcooked and solid.) Transfer to the warm ramekins. Top each portion of scrambled egg with a teaspoon of caviar at the last minute.

Serve with hot crisp white toast.

Serves 4

**Variation**

# SCRAMBLED EGGS ON BRIOCHE TOAST

### WITH BELUGA CAVIAR

This makes a luxury breakfast for a special occasion.

Scramble the eggs as in the recipe for Scrambled Eggs with Caviar (above), and spoon on to hot brioche toast. Other forms of bread may be used if preferred, but toasted brioche has a crunchy texture that is perfect with scrambled egg. Serve with Bucks Fizz, made with chilled fresh orange juice and champagne.

Serves 4

According to regulations in Europe real caviar has to be spelled with a "C" and the cheap imitation with a "K".

## CAVIAR WITH QUAIL'S EGGS

Simply delicious – if you want a more substantial dish, add some smoked salmon.

**3 quail's eggs**

**1 teaspoon finely chopped chives**

**1–2 tablespoons fromage frais or sour cream**

**pinch of ground pepper**

**triangles of hot toast**

**3 teaspoons caviar**

**2 thin wedges of lemon, to garnish**

Bring a saucepan of water to the boil. Put the quail's eggs carefully into a wire basket, lower the basket into the water and boil for 2 minutes.

Drain the eggs and immediately cool them under cold running water. Drain again and gently tap the eggs all around to break the shells. Peel carefully and set aside to cool completely.

Stir the chives into the fromage frais or sour cream with a pinch of ground pepper. Just before serving arrange the eggs and toast triangles on individual plates. Spoon the fromage frais or sour cream mixture over the eggs to coat. Place the caviar and lemon wedges on the plates and serve.

Serves 1

# CANAPÉS

Caviar on canapés is fun and versatile. It can be as impressive or as simple as you wish.

You can let your imagination run from simple toast, puff pastry shapes and mini-pizzas with crème fraîche or sour cream to small new or tiny scooped out baked potatoes...or try one of the recipes below.

The quantities given for these canapés are designed to be flexible – you can simply multiply them to make just the quantity you need.

### Smoked Salmon and Caviar

Slice across enough smoked salmon fillets and then shape the fillet portions into circles or mini-cones, on toast. Pipe a little whipped heavy cream on top and add a small spoonful of caviar.

There is an excellent Swiss fillet of smoked salmon called Balik, if you can obtain it.

### Quail's Eggs with Salmon Roe

Put six quail's eggs into a saucepan of cold water. Bring to the boil and cook for 3 minutes, then drain the eggs and immediately cool them under cold running water. Remove the shells and carefully cut the eggs in half. Toast some bread and cut into 12 small rounds or squares with pastry cutters. Peel a 2–inch length of cucumber, slice thinly and cut the slices in half. Arrange half a cucumber slice on each piece of toast, balance half a quail's egg on top and spoon salmon eggs or caviar on top of each egg.

### Hidden Assets

Take some finely sliced smoked salmon and cut it into rough squares.

Put ½ teaspoon fromage frais or whipped heavy cream and ½ teaspoon Oscietre caviar into the center of each square, gather up into a treasure bag and tie with two chives.

### Lobster Tail with Caviar

Cut a cooked lobster tail into slices. Lightly toast as much white bread as you need and cut it into rounds with a small pastry cutter. Place a slice of lobster (or two) on each toast round.

Top with a few grains of caviar. Alternatively, pop one salmon egg on top with some finely chopped chives.

### Snow Peas

You can eat every morsel of these tasty filled vegetables.

Buy the smallest snow peas you can find. Blanch them in a saucepan of boiling water for 30 seconds, then drain, refresh under cold running water and pat dry on paper towels. Trim, split open down one side and fill with fromage frais and caviar.

In 1927 Cartier had in their brochure a caviar taster, which was a small gold or crystal ball decorated with stars. This was intended to be kept on a watch chain and whenever caviar was served you dropped the ball into it. If the ball sank to the bottom, you judged it good, and if it stayed in the middle, you sent it back!

# CHILLED CAVIAR VICHYSSOISE

Make the vichyssoise the day before you need it, or use a good quality bought vichyssoise.

**¼ cup/½ stick butter**

**6 large leeks, white parts only, washed, trimmed and finely sliced**

**4 white onions, thinly sliced**

**I quart water**

**I quart clear chicken stock**

**6 potatoes, about 6 ounces each, cut in large dice**

**scant 2 cups heavy cream**

**½ teaspoon salt**

**2 tablespoons finely chopped chives**

**I teaspoon lemon juice**

**⅔ cup sour cream**

**8 teaspoons Oscietre caviar**

**freshly ground white pepper**

Melt the butter in a large saucepan, add the leeks and onions and cook gently for 10 minutes, stirring occasionally, until the vegetables are soft but not colored.

Add the measured water, chicken stock and potatoes. Bring to the boil, then lower the heat and simmer for 15–20 minutes until the potatoes are almost tender. Add the heavy cream and simmer for 5 minutes. Purée the contents of the pan in a blender or food processor, then press through a strainer into a large bowl. Add the salt, with pepper to taste. Allow to cool, then cover and refrigerate for at least 2 hours. Just before serving stir in the chives and lemon juice. Pour the soup into 8 dishes, add a dollop of sour cream to each and top with a teaspoon of caviar.

Serves 8

# MOUSSELINE OF CAVIAR, SALMON AND HAKE

**10 ounces salmon fillets, skinned**

**8 ounces whiting or cod fillets, skinned**

**2 egg whites**

**I cup heavy cream**

**about 5 teaspoons Beluga or Oscietre caviar**

**Tomato Coulis (see page 63)**

**salt and freshly ground black pepper**

Pick over the fish to make sure that all the bones have been removed, then cut into chunks and purée with the egg whites in a blender or food processor. Stop the appliance at frequent intervals to clear the blades and ensure that the mixture at the sides is brought to the center. When the purée is smooth, rub it through a fine strainer into a bowl set in crushed ice. Add salt and pepper to taste.

Gradually beat in the cream, adding about a spoonful at a time. (This can be done in a food processor but be careful not to overwork the mixture or it will separate.) Chill the mixture in the refrigerator for 20–30 minutes, to thicken slightly.

Butter 6 ramekins or timbale molds and, using a teaspoon, half fill them with the mixture. Then, using the back of the spoon, make a dent in the mixture and fill with caviar. (If you have any caviar left over, save it for adding to the sauce.) Spoon the rest of the fish mixture carefully into the mold to cover the caviar, turning the mold around as you fill it to just below the rim. Wrap the molds individually in plastic wrap. Put the wrapped molds in a saucepan large enough to hold them in a single layer. Pour in enough boiling water to come about three-quarters of the way up the molds. Simmer for exactly 8 minutes – no longer or you will cook the caviar!

To serve, invert the cooked mousselines onto 8 serving plates and surround with tomato coulis.

*Serves 6*

# SEVRUGA CAVIAR TOPPED POTATO PANCAKES

When it's dark and the weather is bad, potato pancakes topped with salmon and caviar or quail's eggs make a sublime appetizer, brunch or supper dish – nutritious and not too heavy. The quantities given are for one; simply double or quadruple them to serve two or four.

**I small potato, about 4 ounces**

**¼ red onion, grated**

**I egg yolk**

**olive oil for frying**

**salt and pepper**

Topping

**2 tablespoons crème fraîche or sour cream**

**2 ounces smoked salmon, diced**

**I or 2 quail's eggs**

**2 teaspoons Sevruga caviar**

Peel the potato and grate raw into a bowl. Add the onion and egg yolk, with salt and pepper to taste; mix well. Heat a little olive oil in a skillet. Using all the potato mixture, form two potato pancakes (like a hamburger). Fry in the oil over a low heat for 5–8 minutes on each side, until golden brown. Remove from the pan and drain on paper towels. Transfer the pancakes to a plate and keep warm, but not too hot.

Spread one potato pancake generously with the crème fraîche or sour cream. Top with the smoked salmon. Heat a little more oil in a small skillet. Carefully break the quail's egg or eggs into the skillet. Fry the eggs – they will cook very rapidly and should be served with runny yolks. Put the egg or eggs on the remaining pancake. Divide the caviar evenly between the pancakes. Serve immediately.

Serves I

# SMOKED SALMON WITH FRENCH BEAN SALAD
## AND SEVRUGA CAVIAR

**10-ounce fillet of smoked salmon (preferably Balik)**

**5 ounces (scant 1 cup) French beans, trimmed**

**1 tablespoon wine vinegar**

**1 tablespoon lemon juice**

**½ cup olive oil**

**2 shallots, finely chopped**

**12 teaspoons Sevruga Caviar**

**salt and pepper**

Cut the salmon crosswise into thin slices, allowing three pieces per person. Set aside. Blanch the French beans in a pan of boiling water for 1 minute, drain, refresh under cold water and dry on paper towels.

To make the dressing, whisk the vinegar and lemon juice together in a salad bowl. Gradually whisk in the olive oil, with salt and pepper to taste.

Add the shallots. Cut the beans in half and add them to the salad bowl, tossing to coat them in the dressing. Cover and marinate for 30 minutes to bring out the flavor and allow the onion to soften.

Using a slotted spoon, mound the bean mixture on one half or in the center of 8 individual plates. Complement each plate of beans with three pieces of salmon. Just before serving add half a teaspoonful of caviar to each salmon slice.

Serves 8

The Swiss and the French eat the most caviar:
the Swiss because they think they should,
and the French because they love it.

## SPAGHETTI WITH CAVIAR AND ASPARAGUS

1 tablespoon oil

1 pound spaghetti

1⅔ tablespoons butter

⅔ cup light cream

8 ounces asparagus spears (frozen asparagus is fine), sliced

8 ounces smoked salmon, cut into small pieces

5 teaspoons Sevruga caviar

salt and pepper

Bring a large saucepan of water to the boil, adding a teaspoon of salt and the tablespoon of oil. Cook the
spaghetti for 8–12 minutes or until *al dente*.

While the pasta is cooking, make the sauce. Heat the butter, cream and asparagus in a nonstick saucepan.
Add salt and pepper to taste. Bring to simmering point and turn off the heat. Stir in the salmon.

Drain the pasta in a colander. Tip it into a bowl and add the sauce. Toss lightly. Top with caviar and serve
at once, preferably with a rough country bread.

Serves 4

# SANDWICH WITH PRESSED CAVIAR AND CRAB

**12 slices of thin white bread**

**12 teaspoons pressed caviar**

**7½ ounces crab meat, preferably Russian whole crab meat (Chatka Crab Royal)**

**6 tablespoons crème fraîche or sour cream**

**6 dill sprigs**

**lemon slices**

Lightly toast the bread. Spread the pressed caviar thinly onto the toast; trim off the edges neatly.

Top six of the slices of toast with pieces of the whole crab meat. (This can be a delicate operation needing some care and attention to keep the crab meat pieces whole.) Top the crab meat toast with the remaining toast spread with caviar, caviar–side up.

Garnish each sandwich with a tablespoon of crème fraîche or sour cream, a few dill sprigs and a slice of lemon. Serve immediately or the toast may go soggy.

Serves 6

**"Fresh caviar, with its exquisite taste, needs no further seasoning."**
*Ma Cuisine* Auguste Escoffier

# CAVIAR SURPRISE

Spinach-wrapped fish parcels reveal a surprise filling of caviar when cut. You can serve this as an appetizer, or as a main course with rice and perhaps stir-fried snow peas and baby corn to add color and sweetness. We like the tangy wine and butter sauce as it is, but you may prefer to cook and purée any remaining spinach and add this to the sauce.

**4 fillets of lemon sole**

**8–12 large spinach leaves (see method)**

**6 tablespoons/¾ stick butter**

**5 teaspoons Sevruga caviar or pressed caviar**

**Tangy Wine and Butter Sauce (see page 63)**

**freshly ground black pepper**

Slice each lemon sole fillet lengthwise down the center, then cut in half crosswise to give 16 pieces. (Trim off all the ends and add to the sauce.)

Bring a large saucepan of water to the boil. Wash the spinach leaves well, and trim them to remove any tough stalk ends. Blanch eight large leaves (or more, if the leaves are not large) for a few seconds. Immediately drain and plunge into cold water to prevent overcooking. When cool, dry on paper towels.

Preheat the oven to 425°F. Melt the butter in a small saucepan and add generous amounts of pepper.

Using a pastry brush, butter the sole on both sides. Reserve the remaining butter.

Take a piece of sole and gently spread it with caviar; place another piece of sole on top to make a sandwich. Then wrap this in a blanched spinach leaf to make a parcel. Use the reserved butter to grease an ovenproof dish large enough to hold all the parcels in a single layer. Place the finished parcel in the dish, then make seven more parcels in the same way. Cover the dish with foil and bake for 10–15 minutes, until the sole is cooked through. Divide the parcels between 4 plates, pour the sauce on top and serve.

Serves 4

# SEA BASS WITH A CREAM AND CAVIAR SAUCE

1½ pounds fillets of sea bass or sturgeon, skinned

⅔ cup fish stock or water

½ cup dry white wine

1 pound fresh pasta, preferably tagliolini or linguini

parsley sprigs, to garnish

Sauce

2 cups heavy or whipping cream

1 cup/2 sticks butter, diced

juice of ½ lemon

3 teaspoons Sevruga caviar

salt and pepper

Place the sea bass or sturgeon in a shallow pan. Add the fish stock or water with the wine and a pinch of salt. Bring gently to simmering point, then remove from the heat, cover and allow to stand for 5 minutes. Bring a large saucepan of salted water to boiling point, so that it is ready to receive the pasta after you have made the sauce.

Heat the cream in the top of a double boiler. As soon as it comes to the boil, remove from the heat and briskly whisk in the cold diced butter, a little at a time. When the sauce is smooth, add the lemon juice and season with salt and pepper. Keep the sauce hot over simmering water.

Add the pasta to the boiling salted water. Cook, stirring occasionally to prevent the pasta from sticking, until it is *al dente* or according to the package recommendations (about 4 minutes). Drain well and then mound on 4 plates. Stir the caviar gently into the sauce and pour over the pasta. Drain the sea bass or sturgeon and add a portion to each plate. Garnish with parsley and serve with a crisp dry white wine.

Serves 4

# SEAFOOD SALAD WITH CAVIAR

8 small new potatoes

2 small cooked lobsters, weighing about 1 pound each

butter, for frying (optional)

½ garlic clove, chopped (optional)

2 tablespoons white wine vinegar

6 tablespoons light olive oil

about 6 cups mixed salad leaves

8 ounces smoked salmon

5 teaspoons Sevruga caviar

8 tiny cherry tomatoes, halved

5 teaspoons salmon eggs

1 tablespoon chopped dill

salt and pepper

Cook the potatoes in boiling salted water for 10 minutes or until tender. Drain and cool, then cut in half.

Shell the cooked lobster, discarding the intestinal tract. Remove the tail and claw meat.

Serve the lobster cold, or sauté gently in a little melted butter and garlic for about 2 minutes. Take out of the pan with a slotted spoon and allow to cool on paper towels. Whisk the vinegar, salt and pepper in a bowl. Gradually whisk in the oil. Toss the salad leaves in this dressing.

On each plate arrange a thin layer of dressed salad leaves. Cut the smoked salmon into ribbons with sharp kitchen scissors and arrange on top of the salad. Place the lobster meat around the rim of each plate. Arrange the potato halves in between and top them with the Sevruga caviar. Garnish with the tomatoes. Spoon a quarter of the salmon eggs into the center of each plate and sprinkle dill all over. Serve immediately.

Serves 4

# SMOKED SALMON AND CAVIAR PANCAKE

Halfway between a pancake and an omelet, this makes an ideal light dish when served with a
fresh green salad and hot pitta bread.

**⌐ cup light cream**

**¾ cup all-purpose flour, sifted**

**6 eggs**

**½ cup/I stick butter**

**8 ounces thinly sliced smoked salmon**

**10 teaspoons Oscietre caviar**

**freshly ground black pepper**

To garnish

**8 very thin lemon slices**

**fresh dill**

**sour cream**

Preheat the oven to 400°F. In a heavy mixing bowl or a food processor, beat the cream, flour and pepper
until smooth, then add I egg at a time, beating vigorously until creamy.

In an 8-inch omelet pan with an ovenproof handle, melt the butter over a low heat. Pour in the
batter and cook for 2 minutes, then transfer the pan to the oven and cook until set, about 8 minutes.
Remove the pancake from the oven, cover with some of the smoked salmon and trim. Cut it into 8 slices
and put a thin slice of lemon on each. Arrange on 4 plates. Cut the remaining smoked salmon into ribbons
and arrange around the slices. Make two oval mounds of caviar on each plate, using two non-metallic
teaspoons. Garnish the salmon with a little dill. Serve with sour cream on the side.

Serves 4

# SMOKED OR RAW SALMON TARTARE WITH CAVIAR

This can be made with raw salmon, but unless you are absolutely sure of your source, it is safer to use smoked salmon.

**4 ounces smoked or fresh salmon**

**I lemon or lime**

**I red onion, finely chopped**

**30 rinsed capers, drained and chopped**

**heaping ½ cup sour cream**

**12 endive leaves (optional)**

**5 teaspoons caviar**

**salt and pepper**

**dill sprigs, to garnish**

Cut the salmon into small dice. With a paring knife cut off strips of rind from the lemon or lime, avoiding the pith. Cut the rind into julienne strips and blanch in boiling water for a few seconds. Drain, rinse under cold water to retain the color and drain again. Set aside. Squeeze the juice from the lemon or lime into a 2½-cup pudding bowl; add the salmon, onion, capers and sour cream, with salt and pepper to taste.

Mix well, cover and refrigerate for 30 minutes.

Place a serving plate upside down on the pudding bowl mold. Hold both firmly together, then turn right way up and carefully lift off the bowl to reveal the molded salmon mixture. Arrange the endive leaves around the mold, if using. Just before serving, garnish with the caviar, lime or lemon strips and dill.

*Serves 4*

# TANGY WINE AND BUTTER SAUCE

I tablespoon chopped shallot

15 black peppercorns

scant ½ cup dry white wine

2 teaspoons white wine vinegar

2 teaspoons heavy cream

cayenne pepper, to taste

6 tablespoons/¾ stick chilled butter, diced

Combine the shallots, peppercorns, wine and vinegar in a saucepan, with any leftover fish. Boil until reduced by half. Add the cream and reduce again. Strain into a bowl. Place the bowl in a pan of hot water, add a little cayenne. When hot, gradually whisk in the butter until the sauce is warm, but never boiling, and smooth.

Serves 4

# TOMATO COULIS

6 tablespoons/¾ stick butter, of which ¼ cup/½ stick to be diced and kept cold

2 shallots, finely chopped

I pound tomatoes, skins removed and flesh chopped

½ cup fish stock

½ cup white wine

salt and white pepper

Gently soften the butter and shallots over a low heat. Add the tomatoes and cook for I minute. Add the stock, wine, salt and pepper and simmer for 20 minutes. When the sauce has cooled, rub it through a strainer. When required, reheat and whisk in the cold butter, until all the butter has melted.

Serves 4

# INDEX

**A**merican black, 19
aphrodisiacs, 9
Aphrodite, 9
Aristotle, 8
asparagus, spaghetti with caviar and, 50

**b**eauty treatments, 9
Beluga caviar, 17, 24
Beluga sturgeon, 7, 8, 9
blinis, 30
 caviar with, 28
 with buckwheat, 31
borax, 8
brioche toast, scrambled eggs on, 34
buckwheat flour: blinis, 31
buying caviar, 13

**c**anapés, 38–9
cans, 13
capers: raw or smoked salmon tartare with caviar, 62
Cartier, 39
Caspian sturgeon, 7
caviar surprise, 54
Chinese caviar, 15
Cossacks, 9
coulis, tomato, 63
crab, sandwich with pressed caviar and, 52

**d**rinks, 22

**e**ggs: caviar with quail's, 36
 quail's, with salmon roe, 38
 scrambled, on brioche toast, 34
 scrambled, with caviar, 34
 tête-à-tête, 32
Escoffier, Auguste, 52

**f**ish eggs, 18–19
French bean salad, smoked salmon with, 48

**g**olden caviar, 7, 16

**h**ake, mousseline of caviar, salmon and, 44
hidden assets, 38
history, 8–9

**i**mperial caviar, 16
Iranian caviar, 7, 8

**k**eta, 18

**l**eeks: chilled caviar vichyssoise, 42
lobster tail with caviar, 39
lumpfish roe, 18

**M**alossol caviar, 15
mousseline of caviar, salmon and hake, 44
mullet eggs, 18

**N**ew York, 14
nutrition, 9

**O**scietre caviar, 7, 16, 24

**p**ancakes: blinis, 30–1
 Sevruga caviar topped potato pancakes, 46
 smoked salmon and caviar pancake, 60
pasta: sea bass with a cream and caviar sauce, 56
 spaghetti with caviar and asparagus, 50
pasteurized caviar, 15
potatoes: baked potatoes with caviar, 27
 chilled caviar vichyssoise, 42
 Sevruga caviar topped potato pancakes, 46
pressed caviar, 15

**q**uail's eggs see eggs
*Queen Elizabeth 2*, 24

**R**ussian caviar, 8, 9

**s**alads: seafood salad with caviar, 58
 smoked salmon with French bean salad, 48
salmon: mousseline of caviar, salmon and hake, 44
 raw salmon tartare with caviar, 62
 see also smoked salmon
salmon roe, 18
 quail's eggs with, 38
sandwich with pressed caviar and crab, 52
sauces: tangy wine and butter, 63
 tomato coulis, 63
Schipp caviar, 7, 15
sea bass with a cream and caviar sauce, 56
sea urchin eggs, 19
seafood salad with caviar, 58
serving caviar, 20
Sevruga caviar, 7, 17, 24

smoked salmon: hidden assets, 38
 Sevruga caviar topped potato pancakes, 46
 smoked salmon and caviar pancake, 60
 smoked salmon tartare with caviar, 62
 smoked salmon with crème fraîche and caviar, 38
 smoked salmon with French bean salad, 48
snow peas, 39
sole: caviar surprise, 54
soups: chilled caviar vichyssoise, 42
 spaghetti with caviar and asparagus, 50
spinach: caviar surprise, 54
spoons, 20
Sterlet caviar, 7, 15
storing caviar, 13
sturgeon, 7, 8–9

**t**ête à tête, 32
tomato coulis, 63
trout eggs, 19
tuna eggs, 19

**v**arieties, 15–19
vichyssoise, chilled caviar, 42
vodka, 22

**W**aldorf Astoria, 12
wine, 22
 tangy wine and butter sauce, 63